I0087123

My Year In The Gambia

Written by

Sonia Parry

Arranged by

Sharon Hill, Jean Hill

& Debbie Brewer

THE GAMBIA

Copyright © 2019 Sonia Parry

First published in October 2019 by
Lulu.com

Distributed by Lulu.com

All rights reserved. No part of this
book may be reproduced by any
mechanical, photographic, or
electronic process, or in the form of a
phonographic recording. Nor may it be
stored in a retrieval system ,
transmitted or otherwise be copied for
public or private use, other than for
fair use as brief quotations embodied
in articles and reviews, without prior
written permission of the author.

ISBN-13: 978-0-244-55400-2

First Edition

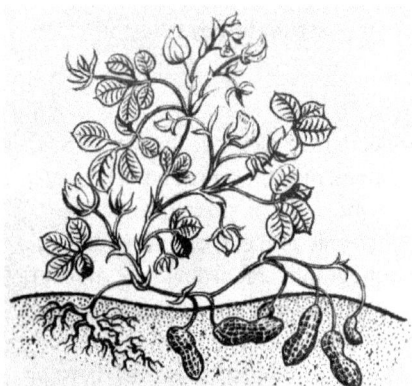

Written for my son, Richard

My Year In The Gambia

Well Richard, you said to me some time ago, that I should put into writing my memories of my year in The Gambia, so here we go.

It had always been my ambition to work abroad and, when I was told I could not sit my finals in Haematology because I was two weeks short of the qualifying time, I decided to apply to Voluntary Service Overseas to travel for a year.

8

I was called to attend an interview in London, I was accepted, then had to wait until they told me where they were sending me, and it was The Gambia.

I left in February 1966. Believe it or not, at that time I had never been on a plane so it really was a big adventure. So much so that two weeks before I was due to go I had a panic attack and told my mother I would not go. She sat me down, talked to me, and told me how much I would regret it, etc., so I started packing.   I also attempted to pass my driving test before I went as I was told this would be an advantage. On my first lesson I asked the instructor to put me in for the test; he was a bit amused but, because of the situation, he agreed to do it. I sat my test after about six lessons, did a reverse around a corner and knocked over three dustbins so that was the end of that.

My Mum and Jean came up to London with me the night before I was due to fly. There were lots of hugs and tears at the airport, but then I walked onto the plane. A bit later it was announced there was a fault in the plane and we all had to get off. Luckily I met up with Mum and Jean again, had to wait a couple of hours, then, again, more tears and hugs, but this time the plane took off. I was on my way.

We landed at Lisbon to re-fuel – long time ago Richard – and then we took off. Another announcement. There was a light in the cockpit which showed there was a fault with the undercarriage, indicating it had not come up. The pilot didn't know if it was a faulty light or if the undercarriage had stuck. It was dark so we had to fly over the runway with lights shining up and people standing underneath trying to see the undercarriage. They thought it was OK so we flew on to Las Palmas where we landed with a line of fire engines and ambulances on both sides of the runway. I can remember being quite excited about it all, didn't enter my mind that we would crash … but we landed safely. Then another announcement, the pilot would not take that plane back up for the last part of the journey so we had to spend the night in Las Palmas. We were all taken to a hotel; my first time abroad! The cabin crew, realizing I was on my own, asked me if I wanted to spend the evening with them and the crew which was nice of them. Didn't pay a thing, it was all on their expenses. We eventually flew out about mid-day the following day. The cabin crew, by now knowing why I was on the plane, once we were over The Gambia, asked me to go up into the cockpit; rather scary. I spoke to people in Air Traffic Control as well; it was great.

Stepped out of the plane into a wall of heat and humidity; never experienced anything like it. I was met by an official from the British High Commission, the pathologist from the hospital I was going to work in, and a girl called Paula, an 18 year old from Oxford, a fellow VSO who was working as a teacher. We were driven to Bathurst the capital, now known as Banjul.

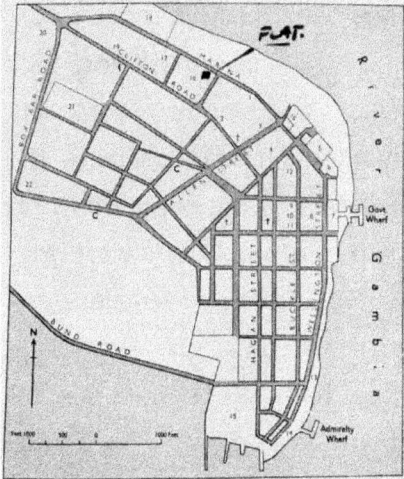

PLAN OF BATHURST

I was sharing an apartment with Paula in a building which had been the Old Military Hospital. It was a nice apartment, high ceilings and wooden floors, very colonial. It was opposite the residence of the Prime Minister! In the flat next door were four boy VSO's, two teachers, an architect and an electrician. They had all been there for about five months. We all shared a cook – Momadou – and a washerwoman/cleaner – Fatou. We all met together for evening meals which was good. They were all giving me information about the place, the people, the climate, the wildlife

– snakes, spiders, monkeys, etc. Tried to take it all in!

Bathurst, the capital of the country, is really a town of two halves, the European side, with its brick buildings, tarmacked roads, and the African township, corrugated buildings, narrow streets, open drains, no lighting. I was invited to the township on a number of occasions, once to a wedding, another time to a festival, and I loved it. You would come across cows, drummers, witch doctors, wrestlers, brides, chieftains, all in one visit. I often went to bed hearing the sound of the drums. Very atmospheric.

We lived on the first floor, overlooking a lovely beach. The Atlantic waves would come rolling in so had to be a bit careful when you went in the water, but it was amazing. There were lovely beaches all down the coast. I used to cycle to my favourite about two miles down the road. I had to walk down a narrow path at the end. There was always this big snake curled up in the same place every day. The first time I saw it I froze, but it just looked at me and stayed there, so I carried on. I think I would have worried more if the snake had not been there in the end, worrying about where it might be!

I started work two days later in the path lab of the Royal Victoria Hospital, Bathurst. I was told I could walk across the grassy area at the back of our block to a gate and straight into the hospital grounds which was great. But on my third morning, I just went to start walking and a snake appeared – last time I did that. I took the long way round along the road, but safer.

Dr Hoare was the consultant pathologist, British, but had spent most of his working life in Africa – really eccentric. There were four Gambian technicians, all very friendly, qualified as much as they could be in such poor conditions. I was there to start up a bacteriology department. All that was there was an oven and an autoclave. I was asked to write a list of everything I needed. I handed the list to Dr Hoare, he just went hysterical with laughter. I was then informed that the annual capitation for the whole lab was £80. My list probably cost about £500.

In the Gwent at this time we had disposable syringes for collecting blood. Here they had 2x5ml and 1x10ml syringes and three needles and a tray of boiling water to sterilize the items in between patients. In one session they might collect blood from 250 patients, a nightmare. No blood bank. If they needed blood, the technician had to go and find a relative and ask them if they were willing to give a pint of blood! No food was provided for the patients; that was left to relatives to bring in. The technicians did a lot of the diagnosing of malaria, parasites, anaemia, etc. It was quite frightening.

One of my first requests once I had set up the lab into some sort of capability, was to test the water supply. A water purification system had been installed about six months before I arrived so the Health Department wanted to know what difference it had made. Well, I tested the water for contamination and found it to be quite bad. This was borne out by the fact that there really hadn't been any improvement in the health of the inhabitants. The authorities were really annoyed as it had cost a lot of money. They called in the company to complain. The company sent engineers to examine the system. It was then discovered that although the system had been installed, no-one had turned the thing on! I was thanked by the Health Department for my work.

During the first couple of months there I was told about a young child in the hospital. She was about 2 years old and had lived all her life there. Her mother had died in childbirth and no-one knew who she was. So the child had just been brought up on the ward, living on scraps from other patients, clothed by other patients. She couldn't really talk or stand as no-one spent much time with her. I asked for permission to take her out a couple of times, which I did, but it was hard because they had no pushchair in the hospital that I could borrow and she was quite heavy to carry. But I took her to meet all the other VSO's and she was spoilt on those day I can assure you.

But at a later date I went to the other hospital in the country in a place called Bansang – 'up river'. There things were REALLY BAD. I had been invited up to stay with the Ceylonese doctor and his wife. They took me around the hospital, no windows, hole in the roof of the theatre, so nothing was sterile. No blood bank and no way of cross-matching the blood to find the right group. If a person was dying for lack of blood, they asked a relative to donate a pint, gave it to the patient in the hope it was the right group; if it was not then the patient died!

The doctor begged me to go and work there and set up a blood bank but I realized that there would just not be enough funds available.

While I was there the doctor took me to a leper colony. When a person was found to be a leper the whole family would be moved into the colony. A man was introduced to me, I shook his hand, and looked all around the village, a bit depressing but a lot of the people looked quite happy. When we left the doctor remarked how brave I was to shake the man's hand. I asked why. I was told he had leprosy and it is catching. I wasn't being brave, just silly, I didn't think. He kindly gave me a list of the symptoms when I left – just in case!

Although I had failed my driving test in the UK before I left, it would have been helpful to be able to drive in Gambia. A British retired doctor who had come there to do a couple of years voluntary work before finally giving up, often asked me to drive him out to the African villages to attend his surgeries.

These really were the real thing – mud huts, no roads, wells, no electricity, cows wandering around the streets, everybody in traditional dress, chieftains, fabulous. It was pointed out to me that if I passed my test in Gambia I could then apply for an International Driving Licence which would enable me to drive on UK roads for a year without a licence, so I applied for a test. I had done a bit of driving there, sometimes without a licence holder. The police knew I did not have a licence so often stopped me. I just had a pile of two-shilling pieces with me, would give them one, and they just waved me away, but it was getting expensive.

A colleague offered to lend me his car for the test. It was a left-hand drive, column gear control car. His driver arrived with it and explained that there was a problem sometimes with getting the car into second gear. But he said he would sit in the back and if I had a problem he would lean over and put it into gear for me. I said I didn't think that would be allowed but he seemed convinced it would so off we went. Much to my horror the examiner was the Chief of Police for the whole country. He sat there with full uniform on plus all his medals! He seemed about seven feet tall and twenty stone. Frightening. We set off. All going relatively well, then the problem with the second gear manifested itself. At this point my back passenger leaned over and started pulling at the gear stick much to the horror of the examiner. There followed a heated conversation in the local language, during which the car went into second gear so I carried on At the next point when I had to put the car into second the whole gear stick just came off in my hand and I was just waving it around in the air yelling "What do I do now?" The examiner looked frightened to death, just yelled back at me "Stick it back in!" So, he was steering the car and I was desperately trying to get the gear stick back onto the column. I managed to do this but the examiner then announced the test could not continue, mainly because I think he was by now very frightened. We were on our way back into town when we passed the hospital and the British doctor I mentioned earlier was driving out of the gate. I quickly said to the examiner that I knew that man, knew the car, and was it possible to continue the test in that car if the doctor was willing. I don't think he knew what I was on about but I managed to flag the doctor down, explain to him what I wanted, he got in the back, and I set off again in a right-hand drive, floor gear control car.

After a while the examiner asked me to take the next available left hand turn, which I did, entering the old township. Very narrow streets, sandy floor, no pavements, etc. He asked me to stop, told me I was in a one way street, going the wrong way. I asked him what I had to do now and he just shrugged his shoulders. There was no way anyone could do a three-point turn there. Just ahead of me was a right-angled turn, impossible to see around it. But there was a man passing us, so I put my head through the window and asked him to walk to the corner and see if there was anything coming, which he did. Luckily no traffic was there so he waved me on. I drove a few yards down that road and eventually came to a decent road. The examiner then looked at me and told me I was not allowed to ask pedestrians to help me drive. I asked him how else I was supposed to get out of that situation, again he just shrugged his shoulders. By now I was just hysterical with laughter. Every time I looked at the examiner I just started laughing. I realized I had failed 'big time'. I laughed even more when I looked in the mirror and saw the poor doctor in the back!

When we got back to the test centre, I stopped the car. He looked at me and to my amazement he told me I had passed. I told him not to be so silly. He said I had driven under very difficult conditions, swapping to different style cars,

I had managed to keep my head together and managed to keep laughing all the way to the end. So I gladly took my licence off him, walked to the man who had lent me the car, who was looking very puzzled as I had not returned in his car. I told him I had passed, he said he knew that. I asked him how and he then informed me that he had bribed the Chief of Police with £5 to pass me. That is when I really went hysterical with laughter.

Anyway I must have made some impression on the Chief of Police. During the test we had passed the only prison in the country and I had asked him about it. A few days after the test he phoned me and asked if I would like to be shown around the prison. I accepted the invitation but he said he would drive! We walked in through big metal gates into a large compound. This was surrounded by single story brick rooms, no glass in the windows, dusty, hot, and two taps in the compound for all the prisoners. They all came out and just stood around looking at me, some with amusement, others just looked blank. No air conditioning, food consisting mainly of rice, a row of vultures on the roof. Horrific. On the way back the Chief informed me that not only was I the first woman ever to visit the prison, I was also the first white person!

Now that I had passed my driving test the British doctor asked me to help him out with a trip he wanted to make. The country of The Gambia is divided into two halves, either side of the River Gambia which extends from the Atlantic right into the interior. A ferry boat travelled right 'up river', a journey which took four days. The doctor wanted to make a

trip to Bansang, the town at the
end of the river.

He asked me to drive his car there, which would take me three days, while he travelled by boat. Then he would meet me, take his car and I would return to Bathurst on the boat.

A fantastic trip which I could not turn down, but it was a bit daunting doing the drive. On my second day of driving a sheep suddenly ran out of the vegetation onto the road. There was no way I could miss it. It was dead. Then suddenly about a dozen villagers appeared from nowhere, all jabbering and pointing to the sheep. I tried explaining what had happened but in the end I took some money out, offered them some and they seemed quite happy, and off they went. But when I looked at the car I was horrified to see water running out of the radiator. Fortunately I had quite a lot of water with me so just about managed to drive to the next village where luckily there was a garage. He examined it, said I needed a new radiator, which he could get for me in about three days. I was horrified as the doctor would be waiting for me. I tried to explain the situation to him, tried to look helpless and upset, and in the end he just went to another car he was working on, took the radiator out of that one, fitted it in mine and off I went as quickly as I could. Had a bit of explaining to do to the doctor when I got there, bashed in front and a few lights missing, etc., but at least I got there.

When we got to Bansang I decided to stay there for a couple of days and have a look around. Again I met the local police who somehow knew I was arriving. I was asked if I wanted to drive even further into the interior as the local police had to 'pick something up'. I agreed but was asked to sit in the back of the open topped van. When we got to the police station two men were led out and put in the back with me and another policeman. The journey took about two hours. When we got back I asked the policeman who the two men were. "Murderers" he said! Oh well, as least I survived.

There were only two cabins on the boat and luckily I had one of them. It was heaving, I was the only white person on it.

Everybody just slept on the deck, wherever they could find a space. One evening I was talking to some of them asking them about their jujus. These are wrapped objects, tied onto their arms, that have been 'blessed' by the witch-doctors which then give the wearer protection from all manner of things. One of them was saying he had a juju to protect him from attack by knife. I was arguing back saying a knife was sharp and a juju could not offer protection. He said if I stuck a knife in him he would not die, so I said the following night I would meet him on deck and stick a knife in him and see who would win. I didn't sleep all night thinking how silly I had been to say something like that. The following evening I went to the deck, didn't take a knife, intending telling the man I had been silly. But he didn't turn up so I think I won the argument!

I got quite friendly with one of the nursing sisters. She was married to a member of the Gambian government. They invited me to spend a weekend at their home. Because he was a Minister he had been allocated a nice home in the country, big gates, very long drive. I had a lovely time, ate lots of Gambian food and they took me to some local villages. They then told me that when the Queen had visited Gambia around the time of Independence, because that house could easily be protected because of its location and long drive, she had stayed in that house. Plus she had also slept in the room that I was staying in. So, I have slept in the same room as the Queen – how many people can say that.

One of the porters in the lab came to see me one day. I knew he had four wives. He told me that his Number Three wife who lived 'up river' had just had a baby girl and he wanted to name her Sonia after me – was that OK? I told him I was thrilled. I bought a big bale of material from the local market as a present for the mother. On my trip up river later his wife came to the hospital and I met baby Sonia and had my photo taken with her. Years later, when you were about seven Richard, I received a letter. It had just been sent to Cardiff Hospital but somebody had done some detective work and it had reached me. The letter was from Sonia, now a married women with a little boy. She told me about her life, told me about her family.

SOHO CAMARA Jr.
BANSANG WARD TOWN
% SUNKARU CAMARA
MACCARTHY ISLAND DIV.
17th MARCH. 1987.

My name Sheri,

It is really a pleasure for me to write this letter to you. I only hope that this letter will meet you in a good condition of health. I wonder if you would recall me but seeing the address above you could remember Mr. Sunkaru Camara of Bansang hospital.

I have only wanted to see you in person, but luckily for me I have your long time picture. I have now completed of my education in Bansang Secondary. Goodness, I have also got marriage. My son - called Malick Secka and his father - Ebou Secka. It has been a long time ambition that when I leave school you will take me to your country but instead my husband is here. I would like you to take my one and only one for the reason I said to that who has all his documents write him. It has been some thing my husband has planned long time a go, like it is sure. One who has promised that he will take my husband to Paris but later on he was disappointed, but during their cause of transaction he has made my husband to get all his document. This is why I want him to go first because I am entirely for him and he is for me. He was so. Please Soniah help us both before my husband gets frustrated. He is a professional man and he was back other. My husband in his workshop and also a picture of my son with his Father. Please if you are to help us with regard to the issue. You can send your reply to Ebou Secka my husband which will be a surprise to him for 1987. If that tends no possibility then you can address it to me as stated above because him is my intention. have think of this plan without the notice of him. If still, will cause problem for him to stay there you can help me with a ticket to come and find a job

P.T.O

Below is the address of my husband so that if you are
to reply direct to him is okie to surprise him

Mr. Ebou Seck.
Tailor for Both Men and women.
Bansang Town.

Best wish and regard to your Family.
Greetings from my Family, My husband at Sea and
especially my Father.

Thank you.

SOnia Camara Jr.
c/o Sunkaru Camara
Bansang warf Town
TR - I D.

MR & MRS EBOU SECKA
SONIA CAMARA JR
BANSANG

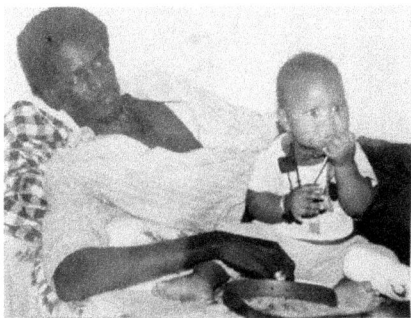

HUSBAND EBOU SECKA
AND SON, MALICK SECKA

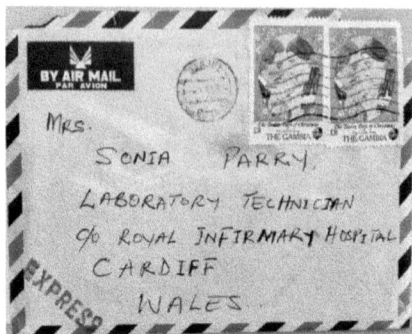

BY AIR MAIL
PAR AVION

THE GAMBIA   THE GAMBIA

Mrs.
SONIA PARRY,
LABORATORY TECHNICIAN
C/o ROYAL INFIRMARY HOSPITAL
CARDIFF
WALES.

EXPRESS

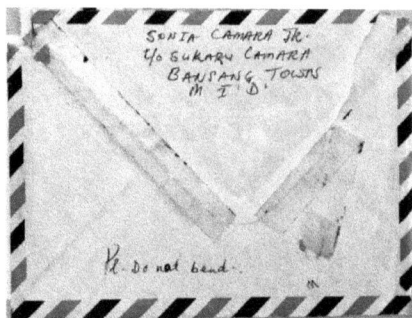

SONIA CAMARA JR.
C/o BUKARY CAMARA
BANSANG TOWN
M.I.D.

Pl. Do not bend.

52

Then said she wanted to meet me; she wanted to come to the UK to live with me and could I send her money for her and her family to come. I was horrified. I would have loved to have been able to reply to her and hear more about her life but I was scared in case she just turned up on my doorstep.

I spent one Christmas Day in The Gambia. By now, the original girl I had shared with had returned home and I was sharing with another three girl VSO's. We decided to do something completely different as we were in Africa. We packed a picnic, borrowed the doctor's car and off we went to explore. We came to a small village and stopped to get some fruit. As usual a few villagers came out to look at us. A little boy told us about a small lake nearby which was supposed to have a crocodile in it and asked us if we wanted to see it. We presumed it was just a way of him making some money so off we went with him, walking through the undergrowth. We eventually came to the lake, stood there looking at it and all of a sudden the boy started yelling and pointing and, there, not too far away, was the biggest crocodile I have ever seen.   He just ran quickly, followed by us.   When he reached the village he ran down the road screaming, everyone came running out of their huts. Apparently the crocodile was not seen very often so people thought we had something to do with it and looked at us in awe. We thought we had better make a quick retreat at that point. We drove off but not too far ahead as the car got stuck in a sand-drift and we had to dig ourselves out. In the heat of the day we got quite exhausted so we spent the rest of the day relaxing on a fabulous beach that we came across.

I am sure the four of us will always remember that Christmas Day.

After I had been in The Gambia about a month the six of us decided to hire a boat and travel up the River Gambia. We hired a motor boat which was just a big trunk that had been hollowed out, a real 'native' boat. We just hoped it was water proof! We visited James Island in the mouth of the river. This was an old settlement, had a castle, used in defence, and the island was also where they used to keep the slaves before being transported to ocean going ships. We then travelled further up river and reached the village of Juffure. I don't know, Richard, if you have ever read the book or seen the TV series 'Roots'. It was written by Alex Haley, a true story of his ancestor who had been snatched from the village and taken as a slave to the Caribbean. It was awesome to go to that village where there was such a strong history of slavery.

The next village we came to was Albreda and, as we pulled up, again the villagers came running to the bank to see us. A man came, holding his young daughter who was screaming, looking at us, obviously frightened. He explained that she had never seen a white person before and asked us if we would touch her, smile at her, let her touch us and be kind to her, so that in the future she would not be afraid of white people. Such a change from what had happened in Juffure centuries before!

Almost at the end of my stay, the country was holding its first Opening of Parliament, run along the same lines as the British system. The country had been given Independence just before I arrived. I managed to get a ticket to the ceremony. It was due to start at 2pm so I got there just before to find my seat. Hardly anyone was there. About an hour later people started to arrive. Eventually, about 4pm, the Prime Minister – our neighbour – arrived and took his seat. All the village chieftains had arrived and were then allocated their seats, equivalent to our House of Lords. Then a big argument followed because one chief wanted his body-guards to be seated next to him but there was no room. Then other chiefs stood up complaining to the Prime Minister that they had voted for him because they had been bribed but they had not received the cows and goats that they had been promised. It was absolute chaos but luckily the Gambians, although very noisy are not usually violent so it all ended peacefully. But it was certainly interesting, quite like our parliament, I suppose.

There weren't many 'proper' shops in Bathurst. Most things were imported, brought by HMS Appapa once a month. There was always excitement when it was due as the shops usually started running out of things by the end of the month. On one visit all the VSO's were invited on board for a wine and cheese evening. I started talking to the Captain, who recognized my accent. He then announced he was from Pontypool, which was amazing. He invited me to lunch on board the following day. What an experience. I was 'piped' on board, escorted by a sailor in full dress to the Captain's cabin. Table all adorned with silver and gold, it was beautiful. Had about three waiters attending us and the food was delicious, quite a change from the food I had got used to eating in Gambia. It certainly showed me how the other half lived for a little while.

Although not part of my stay in Gambia, my journey home was quite eventful too, so I think deserves a mention.

I could have flown home via the same way I flew out, but one of the male VSO's who returned earlier than me discovered that if you flew into an airport and wanted to continue your journey on another flight, if there was no flight available they had to put you up in a hotel. Remember this was the 60's – not so many flights as there are now. So I decided to fly to Senegal, where I could have two nights free, then fly to Casablanca, another three nights free, then to Paris, and finally London. Acting on information, I knew you could get a coach from Casablanca to Marrakech, a six hour journey, so I decided to do that. I had been told that the best place to stay to experience the real Morocco was Jemma el-Fnaa, the huge market square. I arrived there about 1.00 a.m. A bit frightening, dark, noisy and not sure where I was but, luckily, as I got off the coach I saw a hotel, a real local one; not sure what to expect but I had no option. Only cost me £12 a night – so fine, full of character.

The next morning I walked out into the square to be met by noise, colour, smells, crowds, animals and heat – it was amazing. I was immediately surrounded by men in flowing robes all asking if they could be my guide to show me around. I kept saying no as I didn't think I needed one. I just intended walking around. But I kept coming across very narrow alleyways that looked intriguing but a bit daunting, so I changed my mind. Then a young boy of about twelve asked to be my guide. I thought he was the safest option so went with him. The Kasbahs and Souks, were amazing, selling everything imaginable. The young lad showed me all around then appeared to be going into a quieter area and I was beginning to get a bit worried, kept asking him where we were going but got no answer. I was completely lost so just had to follow him. Then he went up this tiny lane and through a door, beckoning me in – I was now really concerned. I was in his own home. All his family surrounded me, brothers, sisters, then his mother approached, full Moroccan dress, no English, but asked me to sit down. She then started to prepare food and drink for me and all the family just sat and watched me. We managed to have some sort of conversation, miming, pointing, etc. Then she presented me with mint tea, cakes, biscuits, meats, salad, etc. I just had to eat it, hoping it was not going to make me ill, but it tasted lovely. I just hoped I had enough money to give her if I was presented with a bill. But when I thought it was safe to leave, she asked for nothing but I gave her money and she looked really pleased. When I left the young guide just went to run off, but I managed to catch him and hang onto him until he got me back to the square. I think you would walk around those alleys for years and not find your way back out. But it was an experience.

I intended spending a couple of days in Paris but by the time I got there I had done enough travelling; all I wanted to do was get home. I managed to get a flight to London. At that time my parents didn't have a phone and they did not know I was on my way back. Their neighbour, a Rev. Thomas, had one though, so I phoned Telephone Directories from a box in Victoria Station and asked the operator to look for Thomas in Newport to find the number. It took her about 30 minutes, which she only agreed to do because I told her about my trip. Mum, Dad and Jean were there to meet me off the train about 11pm, by which time I was tired, dirty, grubby, probably smelly, but very happy to be home.

Well Richard, I hope you have enjoyed a few of my memories of my memorable year. I absolutely enjoyed every minute of the twelve months. I think you will agree I had an interesting time and made the most of my stay. I loved the people and the country so much, but I am afraid to return there. Not long after I left the tourism industry started, hotels went up and took over the beaches; the people started to see how the other half lived and wanted more, which changed them. I think I visited the country at its best time, when there was no racial animosity and I could go where and when I liked without fear, and so could the Gambians. The atmosphere was always relaxed and I thoroughly enjoyed my whole stay.

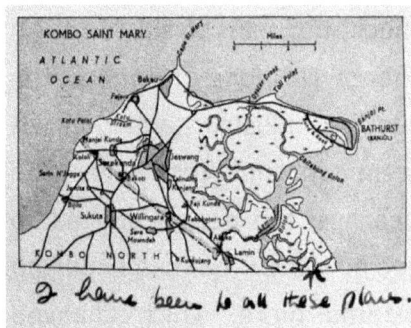

I have been to all these places.

Enjoy my story

Mum

IT WAS WONDERFUL

www.ingramcontent.com/pod-product-compliance
Lightning Source LLC
Chambersburg PA
CBHW071428040426
42445CB00012BA/1289